A Game with Shapes

"Look at me," said Kate.

"I am in

the big yellow triangle."

"Look at me," said Ben.

"I am in

the little yellow triangle."

Ben said to Kate,

"Go to

the little blue square."

Kate said to Ben,

"Go to

the big blue square."

Ben said to Kate,

"Go to

the big green rectangle."

Kate said to Ben,

"Go to

the little green rectangle."

"Look!" said Kate.

"We are in

the big red circle."

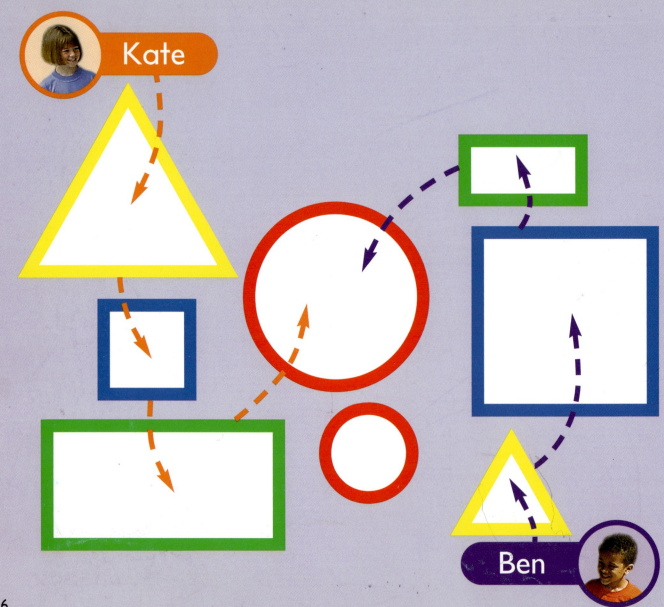